All I Wanted

More books by Jake Young

American Oak

True Terroir: Essays

What They Will Say

For Dorianne and Joe —

All I Wanted

With much gratitude and love for your guidance, mentorship, friendship, and inspiration. May your lives be filled with all you have ever wanted.

♡ always,

poems

Jake Young

Jake Young

2021

REDHAWK
PUBLICATIONS

Published by
Redhawk Publications
2550 US Hwy 70 SE
Hickory NC 28602

Robert Canipe, Publisher and Editor-in-Chief
rcanipe@cvcc.edu
Tim Peeler, Editor
Patty Thompson, Projects Manager

ISBN: 978-1-952485-23-7

Printed in the United States of America

for my brother

Acknowledgments

Grateful acknowledgement is made to the following journals where some of these poems first appeared:

ASKEW: "Burning" and "Water Lilies"

Chicago Quarterly Review: "When the Slack Chain Tightens"

Cloudbank: "Against the Grain"

The Commonline Journal: "Lunchtime at the Farmers Market" (originally published as "Lunchtime at the Farmers Market Reading 'Song of Myself'")

The Hudson Review: "Composed a Few Miles North of Los Angeles"

Lost River Literary Magazine: "Rising" and "In Your Embrace"

LUMINA Online: "Along the Shoulder"

pacificREVIEW: "Wild Fennel," "A Quarter for Your Thoughts," and "The Shower"

PANK: "Harmonic Distortion"

The Sierra Nevada Review: "Before Burn Season Begins," "Hunting Fossils on Shooting Star Trail," "Conversation on the Way to the Market," and "A Place of First Permission"

I would also like to thank my colleagues at the University of Missouri for their careful reading of many poems in this collection, and my mentors and writing professors Aliki Barnstone, Scott Cairns, Cornelius Eady, and Gabriel Fried. My gratitude to the Djerassi Resident Artist Program, where this collection began to take shape during my time as an artist-in-residence. And special thanks and my deepest love to my friends and family—you inspire me.

Table of Contents

Dicebat Bernardus Carnotensis nos esse quasi nanos, gigantium humeris insidentes, ut possimus plura eis et remotiora videre, non utique proprii visus acumine, aut eminentia corporis, sed quia in altum subvenimur et extollimur magnitudine gigantea.

—John of Salisbury, *Metalogicon*, (1159)

Epigraph: (n.) late 16th century (denoting the head of a document or letter): from Greek *epigraphē* "an inscription," from *epigraphein* "to mark the surface, just pierce; write on, inscribe; to register; inscribe one's name, endorse."

Influence: (n.) late 14th century (an astrological term): from Old French *influence* "emanation from the stars that acts upon one's character and destiny." Verb form and meaning "capacity for producing effects by insensible or invisible means" is from 1650s.

I Talk to Myself

When we speak to each other, this
is our conversation—between

you, the whole self, and me,
the aware self: (Somehow

less than whole, but wholly
aware.) When I speak to you,

am I the voice in your head,
or the one who listens?

I Was a Stranger and You

Matthew 25:35

In our haste, we often overlook
our simple, haphazard actions

in the presence of others. We smile
at the shopkeeper stacking boxes

of brown sugar. How sweet we are
in our unthinking. We bloom

as we hold the door
open for strangers, or while leaving

wildflowers tucked into windshield wipers in spring; and

without meaning to,
we embrace the anguish of those

suffering, as we all suffer. Listen
to the scattering of raindrops

against the skylight, the comfort
of a hushed voice,

a damp cloth that wipes away grit
and dried blood—this is how

a touch can suture a wound.
We go forth blessing the world

with every step, offering hope
with each wave of our hand.

Conversation on the Way to the Market

Kill them all, God will know his own.

—Abbot Arnaud Amalri,
during the Massacre at Béziers, 1209

My friend recalls most everything
she learned about the holy wars,

Pope Urban II, the Jews massacred
along the Rhineland, Pope Innocent III,

how the Barbary pirates kidnapped
children to fight as soldiers.

Her bracelets of blue and white nazars
clack like marbles as she speaks,

one hand on the wheel, the other
waving wildly. Our conversation

turns from the Crusades to personal
history. She tells me that the house

where she grew up has been torn down,
paved over for a parking lot. She's seen it,

the last who remembers. So little remains.
Lost are the names of the children

huddled in the darkness below deck,
and the names of the mothers that rang

in the children's trembling voices, sighs
escaping as we avert our eyes from others

on our way to the grocery store,
trying to recall what we need.

The Shower

We're a capital couple are Bloom and I;
He brightens the earth, I polish the sky.
                    —The Soap, *Ulysses* by James Joyce

is this our body?
                    —Gary Snyder, "The Bath"

Water hisses through the showerhead,
warms my neck and back.

I lather my hands with soap to wash them first, a physician
preparing to dissect a cadaver; but instead
of formaldehyde, the scent of jasmine
and lemongrass rises with the steam,
fills my nose, reaches the back of my throat

until my mouth is full of flowers and blades of sweet grass.
I wash my face, blow petals from my mouth, and laugh,
lavish in my flowing gown, a watery grave—
furthest from death that I have ever been

but still close enough to reach out and almost touch it
if I dared. I roll the bar of soap in my hands,
knives against a whetstone, and begin
the dissection of my body: first one arm, then the other.

When I enter the shower I am a corpse on the examiner's table,
cold, stiff, still wandering in the realm of dreams;
when I shower I am the surgeon holding his scalpel,
diving into the body's chasms, feeling about for different organs,
the liver, the kidneys, the testes, the anus, the lungs.

Suds swirl around the drain; everything touched
by water will one day wash away

and we will be left with only the cold light of the stars
and the silent notes of the tombstone blues.

Shower of my nightmares, shower of desire, you are
the cracked shell of a snail
in the corner of the room, porcelain

frame, both entrance and egress,
empty vessel, a form ready to encompass another form,
eager to be entered by another's body.

I scrub the calloused bottoms of my feet.
I've walked to every hospital and bar in town,
and found the water that they offer lacking. Where's the birdsong,
the cricket's chirp that I've grown accustomed to bathing in?

Where is the rainbow of color I wash myself in in the morning
as the sun ascends, peaking through the window,
and the mist burns off outside and rises like steam in the meadow?

Wild Fennel

... the smells and flavors of cooking were likely a prime factor in the development of language.
—Gordon Shepherd, *Neurogastronomy*

After mowing the lawn
I stumble upon a patch

with the overpowering scent
of fennel, so strong

it brings me to my knees,
my head bent low, searching

for the source. This must have been
how early humans first came

to such plants: enamored
by their smell, filled with wonder,

unable to keep from wrapping
tongues around a new sensation.

We were born to recognize
various fragrances, and cannot help

but name what we collect.
And so we learned to speak.

Ode to the Tongue

Dust of water, the tongue
receives through you a kiss
from the marine night
            —Pablo Neruda, "Ode to Salt"

Everything you touch
you praise.
Organ of form, of thirst,
of lubrication, I have
heard you give voice
to the stars, to the ocean
and mountains—

Taste buds, little blossoms,
cover you. Soft
awakening, that first kiss
in the French style,
when we take
another's tongue
into our own mouth,
as we learn how to give
a part of ourselves,
the slick sensation
of tongue against tongue,
of original language.

Caresser of bit cheeks
and chapped lips, fleshy
muscle fleshing out
the mouth's damp
void, forming words
from a single breath.

Harbinger of idiom,
mother of utterance,
you are a flame
leaping in the night.

Without you, songs
would remain wordless,
pages might never be
turned, and we would not
have been able to speak
our world into being.

Rising

The chicken contributes,
But the pig gives his all.
—Howard Nemerov, "Bacon & Eggs"

Hogs roll outside in the dirt, kicking
up clouds of dust; hens strut
and cluck, pecking the ground in search
of scattered grains, a morning
ritual, not much different from my own
slow start. Compost bucket
full again with onion skin
and eggshells; the ripe smell calling fruit-
flies from the ether. Creation's like that:
what arises comes from what already is.
In the cast-iron skillet
on the stove, bacon sizzles in its rendered fat.
I'm careful not to spill the grease
as I pour the drippings into an empty beer
can, the lid cut off, kept in the fridge
beside the egg carton. The pan placed back
on the burner, the heat turned down
low, I drop in two eggs that spit
and hiss, and pour myself
another cup of coffee. When I cut into
the yolk, it runs slowly, the way my muddled
thoughts also slog this morning, bleeding
sustenance into this routine
that's killing me.

Along the Shoulder

for Jeanne

On the road to Missouri lined with black-eyed Susans,
my father murmurs   *these were my mother's favorite flower.*

Summers in Wyoming,   he would gather
handfuls of poor-land daisies for his mother—

she would smile, kiss his cheek,
      and place them in a Mason jar on the table,
           or on the windowsill above the kitchen sink.

It's summer again,
      and the ditches on the sides of the highway
      are full of golden Jerusalems, sunlight
            breaking across
their single black eye and yellow petals—
            a thousand
gilded Temple Mounts in the Old City (millions of prayers
slipped between ancient bricks).   The black-eyed Susans
      turn to the sun. A wild yellow.

Heat Beneath Our Skin

God loves us more than we can stand.
                    —Gary Young, "The bodies of men and women"

There are people who spontaneously combust,
my father told me; a fire suddenly consumes them

from within, and, in minutes, they are left a pile of ash
and bone. Too fascinated to be fearful,

his stories held me, aglow, like light
from a candle's flame. Each day, wonder.

If anyone might unexpectedly burn
without warning—the warmth within our skin,

the desire to live, if it can suddenly be extinguished,
a candle blown out, so that all that remains is a trail

of smoke and the charred scent of sulfur
in the air—then each small discomfort must be

a reminder that there's always more
suffering to come, until there isn't.

Elegy for the Undead

Life is uncertain, death is certain.
—Gautama Buddha

Some nights the light fades,
the trees recede into shadow,
and I worry about the death
of my parents, what to do
with the things they'll leave
behind—the bonsai, masks,
printing presses and type,
all the books, the house
I grew up in, which I hope
they never sell. My father
jokes about having The Poets'
Cemetery established
here on the property, in
the old orchard by his studio,
just a patch of grass now
with a couple apple trees,
one pear, and two plum trees
rotted hollow, somehow still
bearing fruit each year,
so fragile I could push them
to the ground. He's having trouble
breathing again; he's beat
the bronchitis, but this late onset
of asthma… well, "I just need
to get the poison out," he grins,
quoting his own father, who
has just been hospitalized
to have fluid pumped from his lungs.
On nights like these, I imagine
attending funerals, a suit and tie
coal black. And though
I don't believe my father wants to
be cremated, I imagine scattering
his ashes on the land here
surrounded by his old trees,
the buildings he built by hand.

Lost Boys

All my friends are going
And everything just don't seem the same
—The Paul Butterfield Blues Band, "Born in Chicago"

We grew up on stories whispered
in the woods beneath dew dripping
from the needles of redwoods
that draw in fog from the edge
of the bay. The first was a suicide;
just 18, he leapt from Yosemite's Half Dome.
Another, at 22, spun away in a car wreck.
The third, at 25, sank beneath
the warm waves of an overdose.
There weren't that many of us
to begin with. We grew up on stories
of good and evil, were taught to pay attention
to our surroundings, to read the tracks of animals
and their scat along the trails, the danger
of amanita and death caps, the nightmares
that lurk beneath the soil and rise to open
after a soaking rain. We learned to avoid them
on our search for honey mushrooms,
the orange trumpets of chanterelles,
clusters of oysters. We knew where to hunt
for shark teeth in the sandhills,
would spend entire afternoons exploring
Boomer's Castle and the catacombs there,
or the Moon Rocks in the ecological reserve.
How were we to know that years later
a fire would swallow up the trees there
in three-hundred-foot-high flames,
leaving a forest charred black, the ash
carpeting cars and yards like snow?
Below the forest floor where fire raged,
mycelia stretch, swell into the brain-like caps of morels.

How were we to know the stories we were told
weren't meant to save us? We were only boys,
lost in play in the woods, and though we knew
we might one day die, rehearsed that possibility
with a stick for a sword tucked beneath an arm, still,
we could laugh, shake dirt from our shirt, and rise again.

Could Have

What do we know
beyond the rapture and the dread?
        —Stanley Kunitz, "The Abduction"

She tells me she thought she could help
the boy with pink streaks in his hair,
and gauges the size of nickels, who sat
in the back of her first period class
at the high school, the one
she sometimes saw walking
along the dusty backcountry roads
to the trailer park at the edge of town.
She offered him a ride home once.
He had stopped to smoke
on the bridge near the quarry,
and she pulled over to the side
where he stood. He smiled
(the only time she saw him smile).
She asked if he wanted a lift, but he declined,
shifting his weight from one foot
to the other, uncomfortable
in the face of kindness. He stopped
showing up to class not long after.
She still recalls the tattoo of a shamrock
on his left wrist, his dark, green eyes.
At breakfast, eating burnt toast
over the kitchen sink, listening
to the radio, there was news
about a boy found drowned
beneath the bridge by the quarry,
wearing a backpack filled with stones,
and she knew it was him, knew
with a heavy certainty, she could have
saved him that day on the bridge,
offered him a ride anywhere but home.

Our Homes, These Graves

… we die of cold, and not of darkness.
                    —Miguel de Unamuno, *Tragic Sense of Life*

The world is uneasily happy:
It will all be forgotten.
                    —Theodor Storm,
                        from "Goodbye to the Poetry of Calcium"
                        by James Wright

A dog barks at the peal of tires on an icy road.
Beneath the ghostly illumination
of streetlamps, the shadows of barren trees
stretch, still as the bones buried
in the cemetery beyond the border of my fence.
Along the porch, thin coils of vines
and the shadows of their fallen leaves
printed in dirt against the adobe
endure, as do the snow-pocked trails of hollow
footprints, the silent remains of the soft
crunch of snow giving in to the weight
of hurried steps. Every crossing guides us
on our way to prayer. Each step we take
moves us closer to another
benediction. It's a new year. Hallelujah.
On this cold winter night, our lonesome
bodies give in to desire, move to the couch
and are slowly captured by light,
while the bones of the dead decay, sink
deeper into the frosted ground, the grinding
melody of their slow erosion
settling into silence beneath the shadows
of pines and weathered headstones.

On Solitude

To be free
is often to be lonely.
                    —W. H. Auden, "In Memory of Sigmund Freud"

the stove has been out for hours.
I am growing old.
A bird cries in bare elder trees.
                    —James Wright, "In the Cold House"

I.

A raven struggles
with the wind in this thick mist
that clings to the hills
so densely I can hardly see
the first line of trees
through the window. A fire burns
in the wood stove;
I feel its heat on my chest
and my shins and my shoes.
The stove's iron door is latched,
but through the open vent
I can hear the low roar of flames
stripping away at the logs
that burn white and orange,
a hidden iridescence
caged in a black box,
escaping into the air as smoke,
into the room as heat.
So many terrible things
I have thought and said—how
could they ever be forgiven?

II.

On the far ridge, a single pine
barely visible today
braces itself against the wind;
a solitary raven lands
on one of the lower branches,
alert, steadfast despite
the coming storm. This
solitude feeds not on
the separation or sadness
of an intellectual mind,
as Montaigne proposed,
but on introspection; it is
a raw sap that sustains,
that forces wounds to heal.
Alone, there is a release
of identity, a slow peeling
away, birch bark stripped
from the trunk, the wood
bare, exposed, vulnerable,
but fresh as ever,
ready to greet the axe,
ready to meet the flame,
ready to rise as ash and be blown
beyond the furthest ridge.
Long after the fire goes out
the house grows cold,
and only the cry of the raven
wrestling with the wind can be heard.

Sarcasm

n., 1570s, from the Greek sarkazein, *literally
'to strip off the flesh', so it could be eaten.*

Montaigne tell us
that the Caribs tortured
their prisoners of war
before eating them,
and believed
they gained the power
of those they devoured.

Mothers smeared
their breasts
with their enemies' blood
so that even their babies
could drink
and grow stronger.

It's unclear
what Montaigne thought
of such practices.

Old Soul

Old men were once young, but it is uncertain
if young men will reach old age.
                              —Democritus

I've been told that I have
an old soul. This notion
has always seemed silly
to me—if I have a soul,
how could it be any older
than my body? But if it could,
and if souls are immortal,
then how do they come
into existence in the first place?
Wouldn't every soul be
just as old as the next?
At night, I like to sit outside
and look at the stars.
Sometimes I imagine
what it would be like
to be as old as they are,
to burn so hot my light
might shine across the universe
and last long after
I've been extinguished,
and though I don't believe
in miracles, it's a miracle
I've made it this far.

Water Lilies

I must have flowers, always and always.
—Claude Monet

The wildflowers are in bloom.
A falcon hovers
above my car before we both
speed off in opposite directions.
When I return home,
the koi are swimming
beneath the lily pads, the lilies
opened to the sunlight.
Wild iris line the mountain trails
beside bluebonnets and
forget-me-nots. I'm reminded
of Monet's paintings—
his brilliant irises opening
themselves to his touch,
his lily pads that drift
with the breeze, his dreams
engulfed by color even
as his eyesight was failing
and his brushstrokes
no longer covered every inch
of the white canvases.
Like him, I must always
have flowers. The koi today
are like roses under water.

Rembrandt in America

You buried two wives and three children
and wandered the levees in plague time,
sketchbook under one arm
                    —Joseph Millar, "Poem for Rembrandt"

A painting by Rembrandt not only stops the time that made the subject flow
into the future, but makes it flow back to the remotest ages. […] He thus
discovers why, at every moment, every event is solemn: he knows it from his
own solitude.
                    —Jean Genet, *Something Which Seemed to Resemble Decay*

In wooden frames, his
portraits hang as bodies
in open caskets. Beside each
temporary grave, a placard serves
as a headstone: Rembrandt van Rijn,
Titus, the Artist's Son. The shadow
of his cap obscures his eyes, but cannot
hide his youthful confidence,
the cause, perhaps, of his father's
sallow complexion the year before,
his sagging cheeks and sorrowful gaze
in *Self-Portrait, 1659.*
The artist's use of shadow
provides the impression
of detail: Rembrandt,
wearing his burgundy beret,
feverish at his easel, absorbed
by the interplay of light
on his own weathered hands,
the paint poised on his pallet knife
wet and malleable, the canvas
as alive as he is.

I Devour Art

Drawing is not what you see but what you must make others see.
—Edgar Degas

As a child I was raised around books
and printing presses. Everything
exhaled solvent and ink.

I watched as books were composed;
and I have since sewn their spines
using a Japanese stich centuries old,

invented long before Saint Augustine
found the monk Ambrose reading
in a most unusual way, in silence

—nothing moving but his eyes.
How different their perceptions
would have been; how similar.

This afternoon I believe I finally
understand what they must have felt.
Ravenous to enter the creation

of another, you too might one day
wander through Madrid, into the Museo
del Prado, and encounter the work

of Francisco de Goya, and also stand
impassive before a painting that once hung
in the artist's dining room, might stare

into the bulging white eyes,
the bloodied nub of an arm caught
in the gaping black mouth of a Titan,

Saturn Devouring His Son.
You too might find yourself inured
to the violence of creation.

Against the Grain

Wobble and blur of my soul, born just once,
That cleaves to circles. The moon, the eye, the year,
Circle of causes or chaos or turns of chance.
                    —Robert Pinsky, "Biography"

My mother taught me
that cleaning is a reclamation
of space, existential revolt
against thermodynamics,
the ecclesiastical
creation out of nothing—
rejuvenation. I rinse the knife.
Water and a steel blade gleam.
Steam bites at fingers; shivers
sing through me, dizzy
with the sensation of noticing.
How cleanly it splits my silence.
Set to dry, the fresh edge longs
to again plunge into the firm flesh
of an onion, pear, or bloody
steak; anything might do.
O gleaming blade
that craves cleaving,
dry in your rack; tomorrow
you will rush through fields
of cilantro, bushels of bell peppers,
you will reveal the stars
hidden inside a lime—
but tonight, sleep and be.
Rest for now and dream
of chaos, clean.

Lunchtime at the Farmers Market

> *Our shells clacked on the plates.*
> *My tongue was a filling estuary,*
> *My palate hung with starlight*
>   —Seamus Heaney, "Oysters"

A burly, white-bearded man
in denim overalls
wipes his blade on a cloth
tucked into his apron string,
and hands me a paper plate
with three glistening oysters.

        I drop a five-dollar bill
into the wicker basket at the end of the bar,
and take a seat in the shade of an elm.

The oyster-shucker sharpens his knife,
      wipes away water, ice,
and broken bits of shell from the counter
      at his stall in the market.

How well he splits the shells in two,
      separates the oyster's foot from its hold
so that the people in line, wearing sun hats,
      baskets hanging from their arms,
can eat something still alive, savor
      the briny taste of the sea's affection,
         the cool sensation
         of the ocean's tongue
         against their own.

Harmonic Distortion

Music is an agreeable harmony for the honor of God
and the permissible delights of the soul.
                    —Johann Sebastian Bach

When I was three, my father asked,
what does James Brown say,
and I shouted, *Ow! I feel good!*

At five, I danced to Bob Dylan's harmonica
on a splintered redwood floor, buckets
placed about to catch the rain

leaking through the roof. The dark,
knotted beams with human faces hidden
in the wood grains looked down at me,

watched me like the boy who lived reflected
in the windows behind the dinner table
piled with magazines, poems, a calendar

with appointments: *teeth cleaning, surgery,*
taxes, Music in the Mountains. In 1993,
after listening to Bach for the first time,

performed in a forested glen, all I wanted
was to run, to persist as pure melody,
a name echoing from someone's lips.

Honeybees

One clover, and a bee,
And reverie

—Emily Dickinson, "To make a prairie"

Naked in the garden,
bees drift
in lazy loops
among marigolds
and goldenrod.
Paraffin wings
sweep through
soft beams of light.
When the bees
find themselves before
the sweetest flowers,
they let the scent
pull them
momentarily
back to earth, fallen
angels ready to bathe
in the dust
of pollen. I
have known
such pleasure,
felt myself
adrift, glamorous
in the presence
of something greater
than my own
naked body,
feet barely held
to the garden's
green grass.

Composed a Few Miles North of Los Angeles

—Once again
Do I behold these steep and lofty cliffs
That on a wild secluded scene impress
Thoughts of more deep seclusion; and connect
The landscape with the quiet of the sky.
—William Wordsworth,
"Composed A Few Miles Above Tintern Abbey"

South on Route 5
the almond trees appear
midway through bloom.
For miles, nothing
but row after row,
branches covered
in small flowers, the faintest
hint of pink in the blossoms.
Between rows, pale petals
have settled
to a blanket of snow, almost
like winter
five years ago, when
Ben and I stopped
at Versailles to walk
the grounds, where a thin
carpeting of white
ran between bare rows
of beech and ash. It was
February, I remember,
and that winter in Paris
seemed to lack any chill.
Today, in California,
March is almost
here, and spring has
already arrived. Poised
at ends of the almond rows,
beehives stacked in piles
of sixteen crates mark
every eighth mile.
I want to tell Ben

that the road here
is lined with almonds,
miles of even rows; and bees
have been trucked in
to pollinate their flowers.
Bees sweep through
branches, traversing
the almond trees,
passing overhead, some
striking my windshield.
First one, then others
thump the glass
like fat drops of rain.
At the storm's edge
the bees disappear,
and then the trees
as rain begins to pour
against the car, sheets
of water falling so fast
the windshield wipers
can't do a thing.
We all cut our speed
in half, slow to a crawl
to follow the red lights
of the car in front, each of us
becoming a guide
for the person behind, each
the lead and partner
in a dance. Rows
of flowering almonds,
stretched and twisted
ballerinas in repose,
shed their remaining petals
to the ground; the rain cleans
the bees from my windshield.
In the distance, in the quiet
of the sky I catch the faint
light of sunset, blossoming
the clouds.

A Rare Bone Disease

Dem bones, dem bones gonna rise again
—Spiritual folk song

Some bones bloom beneath skin, lilac
or rosemary, swollen buds
split open; and yet, this growth
stunts limbs, too, even as bone
grows like wax flowing
down the sides of a candle,
a slow guttering. No one is sure
why; but the pain is real,
the gasp of a rose expanding
within a hip, ankle, or arm,
so intense you cannot look upon it.

And you think you're alone;
the only one with flowing bones,
until you meet someone else
with a bouquet hidden inside them,
petals peeling outwards from shins
or fingers or spine, bones bursting
with calcified blossoms. How beautiful
to find another who understands
the pain that blooms within you
and feel you're not suffering alone
every morning when you wake.

Hunting Fossils on Shooting Star Trail

When you break a fresh slab of oil shale, you can smell the organic echo
of ancient sea life energized by sunshine hundreds of millions of years ago.
—Kenn Kaufman, *Field Guide to Nature of the Midwest*

Two young women and I, almost giddy
at having left our books behind, search for fossils

along the dry riverbed; the sound of their voices
makes the day more lovely, laughter

sown bank to bank, scattering
the dry scrape of leaves and the clack of rocks

tossed aside, rattling like dice.
I show them how to spy the stone

screws of fossilized *Archimedes*,
the cupped indentation of brachiopods,

the spiraled snail shells of ammonites,
the ways a rock can split to reveal a facet

pocked with remnants of life.
My field guide says *the Midwest is*

geologically stable today, but
I'm not so sure. My balance teeters

on leaves from Eastern Hop Hornbeams
and Silver Maples that hide uneven stones.

Long ago this place was *an active*
tectonic zone fissured by large-

scale rifts. On this bright October
morning, I think change still takes place

here, but at a quieter pace. At times
a compressed mind will clash against a thought

with geological intensity.
Beyond our own tectonic shifts,

still pools, remnants of the river, invite
the flattest stones to sail across their surfaces.

I let fly smooth calcified remains.
Swollen with rocks containing shadows

of an ancient sea, my jacket pockets clap
against my knees. I stoop to examine a small

flat piece of polished limestone. At its center,
a shell the size of a pea. The shell itself

is opaque and glints like amethyst. The shell
fossilized, became stone, and then a geode,

as crystals formed where there had been a life,
some creature that once searched the ocean floor.

I thumb the surface once more, and right myself.
We follow the river, beaming, awash in light.

A Place of First Permission

Hearts unfold like flowers before thee
—Henry van Dyke, "The Hymn of Joy"

that is a place of first permission,
everlasting omen of what is.
—Robert Duncan,
"Often I Am Permitted to Return to a Meadow"

I've been reading Craig Arnold's poems again,
        a man who died because he could
not resist exploring an active volcano
        in Japan. Someday, I think,

I would like to go there, the way
        I imagine someday
snorkeling along the Great Barrier Reef,
        or hiking a glacier

in Switzerland or Peru. I imagine
        it's the same for many of us,
wanting what is out of reach but
        within sight, the way we might lust

after a stranger at the opposite end of the bar
        who reminds us of someone
we once knew and who only visits
        now in dreams. Hell,

I've been that person, felt
        myself desired, held
by a look that whispers, I want
        to claim you

for my own. But such leering
        does not warrant a return;
I've given it back and promised
        never to do so again—

though, understand, I might,
      at some point, wanting once more
to be known. The way a body
      of ice moves under its own weight,

so I too move under the weight
      of my own thoughts;
not again, I tell myself, conscious I want
      to be inhabited

again, want to be coral feeding on light,
      a reef home to so many
colorful lives. I tuck my book
      back in my bag,

suck down the last warm sip of beer,
      and follow a stranger's
gaze through the window behind the bar
      to a magnolia tree.

The tree is in bloom, the large flowers
      white with magenta backs.
Somewhere not here, another person
      has stopped what they are doing

to contemplate the magnolia blossoms,
      perhaps in Japan,
perhaps elsewhere. It doesn't matter.
      What matters

is that they are pleased with what they see.
      And knowing this, so am I.
Caught by a breeze, the limbs shake,
      but the petals hold fast.

In Your Embrace

You can come to me in the evening,
with the fingers of former lovers
fastened in your hair and their ghost lips
opening over your body
—Joseph Millar, "Dark Harvest"

Wrapped in your embrace I feel thankful,
        realizing I could love
anyone like this. Which is to say
        anyone is beautiful;
and thank you for teaching me
        how to desire you
feel so much pleasure that you moan,
        cry out, or cannot
make a sound—sheets clutched
        in fists, thighs clenched
around me, my hands on breasts
        held by how many other lovers
I do not know. Nonetheless
        I am thankful for this
sharing of bodies bringing us together,
        and even with the lights off
we can find each other,
        please one another
as we've pleased others, or
        have failed to do in our attempts
to learn what we know now:
        that there are others in bed with us
always, past lovers who move through us
        tangled in the sheets.

In the moments after
    we both come,

while I'm still inside,
    lying on top of you,
your arms wrapped around me,
    you kiss me playfully;
I nibble at your neck,
    softly bite your lower lip,
remembering other lovers
    who showed me how
to wander through a body
    like a forest, discovering
new trails, how to tease
    nipples with my tongue,
reminded me not to stay
    silent while making love,
how every open mouth
    wants something different,
knows a different way to please.

Listen and You Can Hear

Spring passes.... Far down the river now,
I find you alone under falling petals.
                    —Tu Fu, "On Meeting Li Guinian Down the River"

Camellias fall, soft thumps
against the brick terrace,
quiet sighs, shoes dropped
to the ground, pants tossed
to the floor. Spent petals, dry
and brown, give themselves
to the earth. Still, above, red
silken blossoms peek through leaves
glistening among umber branches.
Waiting for your return, I listen
for your footsteps in the distance.

Landlocked

Do you not hear the sea?
    —William Shakespeare, *King Lear*

A warm breeze
bursts through
dry autumn leaves
overhead—the high
crash and spray
of waves churning
against rock; and below,
with held breath,
for an instant
I can feel the cool
northern California sun
press fingers of light
against my shoulders,
slick ropes of seaweed
wrap around my calves,
and I can't help
but wonder, where is
the overwhelming odor
of drying kelp, of air
that tastes of dirty salt?
The gust dies away,
the tide recedes,
but the twisted metal forks
strung up behind me
continue to chime.

In California

for Trillium

We sip oaked chardonnay
and talk about her sister

who's tried to take her own life,
the parent who drinks

too much, of how we feel
helpless in the face

of confrontation—antecedent
to any resolution. We continue

to discuss the uncertainty
of the future. No matter;

we're free for now
to sit here on this deck

overlooking a creek
that hasn't run so high in years.

Thinking About Loss

The air stings
like autumn, clarifies
like pain.
— Robert Hass, "Palo Alto: The Marshes"

Somewhere between her story
about her girlfriend who moved
back into the house where her
husband had overdosed, and that
of her newborn nephew who
suddenly stopped breathing
just before his first birthday, I lose
track of her conversation, my thoughts
staggered and uneasy, pitiful,
and full of pity. She stops a moment
to snap a photo of the lake, which today
looks particularly green, all
except for one small, glinting wound
near the far bank. The first tree
turned toward fall. Maybe a sycamore?
Ashamed of my ignorance, I turn
from the tongue of flame lapping
the water's edge, and walk.

77 Years Later

after W. H. Auden, "September 1, 1939"

I sit in one of the dives
off East Broadway, contemplating
the years since you penned
this opening line.
We've remained *uncertain*
and afraid of the nation's future
as *waves of fear and anger circulate*
through Dallas, Baton Rouge,
Baltimore, Orlando, Charlottesville,
as private lives turn public
and the media feeds off
the odor of death that offends
another summer night.

The faces of the dead stare back
through muted television screens;
faces along the bar
cling to routine: bottles empty
of their own accord,
music softly plays, and
all the conventions conspire
to heighten our basest fears.
From the conservative dark,
dense throngs *repeat*
their morning vow to
make America great again.
Fearful of the strong woman,
the Muslim, and the exile,
politicians promote hyperbolic
rhetoric, *a habit-forming pain*
and the mismanagement of grief.
Obtuse, militant bigots
shout about a greatness
that never was, as police murder
young black men in the streets.

The names of murdered citizens
ring out in frenzied air as pain
washes onto dirty city avenues,
and we wonder, *how long can we live
in this euphoric dream?*
What Havel wrote about dissent
is true: "Not standing up
for the freedom of others
means surrendering one's own."
In this land of incarceration
we are one nation, under
a psychopathic god,
home to the brave and the oppressed,
the hated and the feared,
to every color and creed.
We, a culture driven by madness,
sacrifice values for greed.

You taught me that
all I have is a voice,
which I must embrace if I ever hope
to *undo the folded lies*
that insist hunger doesn't follow
a quarter of our children home,
and it's because we're lazy
that poverty clings to us
(bless their hearts) like our own
filthy shadows.

Auden, we are just as *defenseless
under the night* as when you left us
staggering out after one last pint.
I used to believe love could conquer
fear and hate, but I am no longer sure.
And yet, *beleaguered by negation
and despair,* your *ironic points of light*
still wink from the heavens, a glint
in God's eye, an acknowledgment that
we are all at fault, we are all to blame,
though we might still hope
someday to resolve our shame.

Disinterestedness in Rodenticide

The creature hath a purpose and its eyes are bright with it

—John Keats, letter to his brother and sister,
George and Georgiana Keats, February 14, 1819

Not because I care for death,
    in fact I fear such certainty,
        but because the rats returned,

I'm at this hardware store to buy
    poison, traps, steel wool,
        and lye to reclaim my house.

Here it is: the poison aisle.
    So many different ways to kill
        a snail, a mole, a mouse, a vole,

ants and roaches, ticks and fleas.
    Our pets may judge us
        with sardonic smiles,

for they already know that we
    invented our own demise and
        prize what we cannot attain:

a life free of vermin and
    villainy—these green toxic
        pellets just might work!

For we are vain, and in ignorance
    we invited these creatures
        soon as we settled long enough

to build a home and plant our grain.
    The rats would have come no matter
        what the cost to eat

the food we store. The cats we love
only settle at our feet
because the mice

came to suckle rice and bulgur, rye
and barley wheat. We domesticated
rodents, but they are not

all we imagine
they are. The death
and disease we fear

lives in us. It's time to check out,
I've found my traps
with the wooden base

and a spring in back
to snap their necks. We fear
what we dare not

describe but know is true—before dawn
draws to a close at end of day,
when stars will fall,

and the sun dim as we unlearn
war, and all the violence
that we have wrought

will decay, fade as the day falls on unpicked
apples that rot in the orchard, cores
turned to sod, a pile

of seeds without a body, beyond
expectation, then the luminous
eyes of scurrying creatures

will lure us to unknown places
and we will seek out once again
those we've forgotten were once our friends.

Que Sera, Sera

for Christopher Buckley

Do not be afraid; our fate
Cannot be taken from us; it is a gift.
                    —Dante Alighieri, *Inferno*

In 1956, Doris Day sang
"Whatever will be, will be"
in Hitchcock's new thriller
The Man Who Knew Too Much.

Watched now, knowing that
the assassination attempt
of the Prime Minister will fail,
Day might as well have sang

"whatever will be, has been."
Time, physicists tell us,
moves forward and backward
mathematically. Philosophers,

however, argue whether time is
singular and constant,
a perpetual present, or if
it is expanding, each moment

merely a point along a line.
Because each perspective differs
from the next, "whatever is, is not"
seems to better reflect the concept

that life is full of contradictions,
that we are not some solid self,
but an amalgam of selves
reflected in others,

polymorphous beings
directed by constraints,
like the number zero, we are
what we are not.

And perhaps, if who we are,
like the future,
is not ours to see,
"whatever will be" is enough.

When the Slack Chain Tightens

Consume my heart away; sick with desire
And fastened to a dying animal
It knows not what it is.
                    —William Butler Yeats, "Sailing to Byzantium"

When the slack chain tightens,
the pedals spin, and the gears crank;
the rubber tires go bald
against the asphalt, and the air sings
past my ears. I let go of all
regret. When I'm suspended
above the saddle, riding high
in the stirrups, leaning forward
over the black handlebar,
it's the speed I can't resist.
I am flush, even in winter, racing
home from work, two pints deep
after scrubbing down the bar,
dreaming of dinner, feeling light
as the mist that speckles my glasses.
At the top of the last hill,
I hit the downshift, and coast.
I could almost believe
this body, this sack of organs,
tendon and bone, was meant to fly.

Before Burn Season Begins

The only thing that endures is change.
—Heraclitus

While friends in New York
dig themselves out
of eighteen inches of snow,
here in California I walk
along the seashore, mid-January
in short sleeves, wondering
if it's ever going to rain again.
Cal Fire has cleared brush
inland on the mountain,
and driving along the backwoods
you can see piles of branches
covered with strips of paper, ready
for the rain we need
to begin the burn season.
While we wait to set fire
to dried out Christmas trees,
nature roars on ahead.
Big Sur has burned,
flames licking the ridge
where Kerouac nearly drank
himself to death. I've read
the same philosophers
he studied, a reminder that any
good idea I might have
belongs to others. Nothing is
ever truly lost, only changed
from one form to another, moved
one place to the next—moments
captured as negatives
become photographs I carry
from apartment to apartment:
my father as a child
with his mother when she was
still alive. My mother

in scuba gear, a snapshot
taken by her father the year
before his death. One of me
at the beach with my brother
as boys, collecting sea glass.
Today, I'm free
to walk along that coastline,
listening to the gulls, their cries
that seem to shriek,
I'm alive. I'm alive. I'm alive.

Evidence of Time

The air is cool along the shaded river
path that runs beneath bridges
rumbling with the sound of passing cars.
The paw prints of a raccoon
embedded in the pavement are filled
with last night's rain. Small white flowers
the size of snowflakes wave in clusters
from the ends of thin grassy stems

along the bank; the orange day
lilies have begun to bloom, and so
have the purple flares of garlic chives,
slipping from their buds, miniature
fireworks frozen in midair. I pull one off
with my teeth and chew the spry bloom.

At the coffee shop, a young woman
with short, violet hair is roasting coffee
with the owner, who answers his phone, then leaves
to pick up his son from daycare.

The door to the shop is open, and by this evening
the whole patio smells of roasted beans.

Reunion, El Matador State Beach

Sober, we're together and happy. Drunk,
we scatter away into our own directions…

—Li Po, "Drinking Alone Beneath the Moon"

We settle on a cove at the base of a cliff
twenty feet tall, with iceplant that hangs

over the edge, and squat agave that dot
the thicket above. I search the pack we filled

with liter bottles of artisanal beer, a local IPA,
one infused with jalapeños, a small-batch stout,

a rustic saison, and some of the best medical-grade
pot this side of the Sierras. Ben dries himself

in the sun after a quick dip into the ocean
that glimmers like sardines, while Shay and I

pass a bottle back and forth as we lounge
on a blanket in the sand. I take a sip and hold

within my mouth a most wonderful bitterness
as a flock of eight black cormorants land

on a large rock in the shallows, the last remains
of a past coastline, to preen in the sun. Today

the air tastes of hops; the sand is the color of dried hops,
with its grains of quartz and broken shell, bits

of the fractured world collected together, where
we've collected on this quarter-mile stretch

of beach on a day when everything lingers on
my palate, the combination bitter, fresh, and sweet.

At First

Everything we call real is made of things that cannot be regarded as real.

—Niehls Bohr

I mistake the swallows
for bats
as they titter

and flit about
the smokestacks
and steeple

at the edge of dusk—
the last embers of sunset
ablaze at the horizon—

a stray glance
that alters
this cloudless night.

A Quarter for My Thoughts

*String theory has led theorists to the idea that space and time are illusions. Nature
is like the three-dimensional image on a two-dimensional bank card, a hologram.*

—Dennis Overbye,
"String Theory, at 20, Explains It All (or Not)"

A monarch butterfly lands on a thistle
in front of my studio. Wind rushes past,

rustling through the grass up the canyon. A haze
obscures the horizon, and makes the whole scene

oddly two-dimensional, like a landscape
painted on one of those porcelain dishes they sell on TV

to old folks who order boxed sets over the phone,
or like a silver face on the side of a coin.

I take a quarter from my pocket, and hold it
to my eye. I cover every mountain ridge, hundreds of trees,

shrubs, acres of open fields of grass—all hidden
behind the coin. But when I unfocus my eye, I still see

the green fields speckled with poppies—an illusion,
or hallucination—the whole scene now comes back

into focus on the face of the quarter. I lower the coin,
and there are the hills, the hidden skyline,

the row of spruce and poplars. I flip the quarter into the air,
catch it, and set it on the table beside my chair. If

I can call into question my own perception,
then perhaps my conception of reality is incorrect.

In elementary school, a friend wrote a story about a girl
who found out that only she was real, that everything

and everyone she loved were holograms, and so
she jumped from a bridge. I've always liked the idea

that perhaps everything is an illusion—maybe
we really are one universe among infinite others,

each merely a collection of information
on the surface of a black hole at the center

of another galaxy in another universe.
And maybe all of it—the stars, the ocean,

our own dying, is a projection, a hologram
that can only be seen from the inside,

as if introspection is a requirement
of the laws of physics, and this—introspection,

the orange and black butterfly landing on a thistle,
the quarter on the table—emerges as meaning

that we create, and though this, too, is
just another illusion, it's as real to me as this

gentle warmth, the sun pressing against my jeans,
my legs crossed in my chair, half in light, half in shadow.

Far from Home

Orchids have interested me as much as almost anything in my life.
—Charles Darwin, letters held at Kew Gardens, London

I can't go back to yesterday because I was a different person then.
— Lewis Carol, *Alice's Adventures in Wonderland*

She managed to accrue a little cash
selling off her father's library when he died.

He had always belonged to the sea,
given himself to the formless, briny grind

of waves and the awesome depth beneath
his feeble boat. She can almost hear the scrape

of ice sheets, can almost see her father
rolling up a net like a holy scroll

after he has mended it.
She has left her dormitory, traveled

past forbidden borders, to a country
she thought she would only know in books,

the stories she read as a child, waiting
for her father's slow return,

thumbing through the well-worn pages,
salt scented with sea spray from when

he had carried them on his voyages.
The girl wanders ankle-deep

through a field in Peru, fragrant
with wild orchids, tiny folds of paper,

little candles that flicker in the wind.
She sits amidst the rustling grass

to untie her laces. She removes her shoes,
stuffs her socks into the toes,

and reclines. A steward of dreams,
she shelters memories that reside

in the recesses of time's unyielding
progress. Slant rays of light

wash over the young woman,
her slender legs, crossed at the ankles.

Drowsy, she gives herself over to this
moment's pleasure. When she wakes,

it will be dusk, moon-cool, and
dusted in pollen, she will rise.

Burning

for Dennis Saleh

Driving home from San Francisco,
        still warm from a final sip of port,

I notice lights
        flashing at the top of a hill

just past the road to San Gregorio.
        Orange flames

leap out of the night,
        a thin blaze

below the ridge.
        On the other side

of the road, a single,
        unblinking light

shines at the horizon,
        a button

holding the sea
        and sky together,

in stark contrast
        to the air and the flames

in flagrante delicto—
        a line from the poem

that once hung on my wall,
        a thought that suddenly burns.

Trash Night

How could they see anything but the shadows
if they were never allowed to move their heads?
—Plato, "Allegory of the Cave"

The canyon air
at the top of the drive

smells faintly of drift smoke
blown in on a northern wind.

After I take out the trash,
the blue light of dusk

offers only pale impressions
as details of the world fade

and my mind wanders
among the shadows.

In such moments
there are only forms:

the tree line, a patch
of amaryllis, the imprint

of a house
in the distance.

What the Wind Knows

They do not pray.
If they make a sound it's eaten
by the wind.
> —Dorianne Laux, "The Life of Trees"

Trees envy birds.
They've seen hawks
follow a murmeration,
and with the slightest flick
of a wing tip, boomerang
back in a sharp arch,
an effortless dive,
wings tucked, talons
outstretched to grasp
a starling. When claws
curl around branches,
trees flex their roots.
Jealous of travel,
they long for the quickening
in the birds' hollow bones.
There is an ache in old wood.
Owls nest in ancient oaks,
finding comfort in solid timber.
When sunlight warms stiff bark,
the birds molt, alert, listening
to the dense, fibrous straws,
the sap's slow journey
up the trunk, along limbs
and capillary-thin twigs,
to leaves that luff in the air
like a sail, each tree a boat,
a vessel moored at harbor,
or the harbor itself
where the birds are ships,
and I, filled with envy,
am the trees. And you,
you, my friend,
you are the wind.

While Reading One Day

after Antonio Machado

An idea, one miserable day, rose from the pages
of a book like the scent of jasmine

carried by wind, and sent me adrift. "In exchange
for releasing me from my narrow vision

of the world, I will plant a field of sunflowers," I thought.
But I had no seeds, nor any flowers left.

All my garden… all was wilted or overrun by weeds.
"Then I will turn the plot, enrich the soil

for next year;" but my shovel was rusted through,
and my hoe was nowhere to be found.

"What have you done?" I cried. I was too absorbed
to look after my garden. "What have you done

with the weightless gift entrusted to you?" Gone
from here, life drifts overhead with the gnats.

Shelter Gardens Arboretum

I'd like to tear these petals with my teeth.
— Li-Young Lee, "Irises"

I am not brave at all.
— Gwendolyn Brooks, "Strong Men, Riding Horses"

The cold snap has left
the magnolia blossoms limp and bruised,
    the brown, wilted petals
the flayed skin of heretics nailed to branches.
    Others are more fortunate.
The redbuds, late bloomers, have been spared.
    Last season's empty pods
still cling to branches beside pink and fuchsia buds
    peaking through the bark.
Trails of silk unspool from the tallest trees, wafting
    in the wind; the geometer moths
have attained flight and have no need now to measure
    the earth, inch by inch.
Hollow pods and wilted flowers, the abandoned
    husks of moths, forgotten
monuments to transformation. Beyond
    the small grove of Japanese maples
with mythic names—*Sherwood Flame, Waterfall,*
    Burgundy Lace, Red Dragon—past
the bobbing cups of tulips
    dipping to gather wind,
at the far end of the garden, a memorial has been
    built to honor the soldiers of Vietnam
and the employees of the insurance agency that owns
    this arboretum who served
in Desert Storm. On a wooden bench
    across from rows of names
engraved on copper plaques, I read
    theories about socialism,
fetishism, and the hidden nature of value.

From a distant corner
I hear the laughter of children. They do not yet fear
        their own wilting, how
we all wither and curl. And finally we fall.
        And the flies lay maggots
in our rotting corpse, feast on our flesh. Shelter Garden
        blossoms fill me with remorse.
Will we never be forgiven? No, we should never
        expect anything but ignorance.
Yet I am not discouraged, no, not entirely. Threadbare,
        unraveling, might I not yet stumble
upon a needle and thread; might I not yet
        sew blooms to the lips of every branch?
I rise to follow gravel paths
        and the honeyed scent of viburnum
that hangs heavy on the air, where fuchsia petals
        ripple along the boughs of the redbuds in bloom.
I strip off redbud flowers by the fistful
        and fill my mouth with them, petals stuck
between my gnashing teeth.

Sick Man Looks at Flowers

after Gwendolyn Brooks

but he does not see flowers,   does not notice
the heads of the chrysanthemums
                have drooped,
their white petals browning   at the edges, nor
     that the water in the vase
should be refilled,   nor does he care. The flowers

are not flowers. They are the last small gift
     his children have left him,   his wilting
body, parched, wrinkled,
             waiting to be forgotten,
returned to the earth.
          The chrysanthemums are
his eyes looking over   the empty room.

They see him   as he sees himself.
     Waiting,   what else is there?
Perhaps someone will   drop in
     with wine, he thinks,   some old friend,

or maybe   one of his children.
            Evening arrives,
     but he is not hungry.
         He will make supper
later, he tells himself, knowing
          this is not true.
No one is coming;   no one
     will bring wine   or sit at his table
       and compliment his flowers.

Reading *Sex at Dawn*

after Cacilda Jethá & Christopher Ryan

Independent of Darwin,
Alfred Russel Wallace
imagined struggle

as the mechanism
of natural selection,
experiencing a flash of insight

as he read *An Essay
on the Principles of Population*
by Thomas Malthus (who

was echoing Thomas Hobbes
a century-and-a-half earlier);
and when I read

about the state of nature,
"and the life of man,"
my attention turns,

not to the evolution of thought
in my hands, but to the soft mist
settling on the skylight.

Afterhours

What took me
completely by surprise
was that it was me

    —Emily Bishop, "In the Waiting Room"

The closing bartender
mops behind the bar,
ready to shut off the lights,
ready for her own drink
and soft sheets, ready to slip
between two leaves
rustling in this
early spring air. I exhale
the copper taste of a cash drawer,
the flapped, starched linen
of the final table
flipped for the evening,
the silverware polished
and set in neat rows
below the napkins
stuffed into wineglasses
raised to the stars.
It's long past last call. The stars
are drunk, and we all
wander out. I am
the water
in the empty water glasses,
the flame
in the unlit candles,
earth removed
for the bar's foundation,
and the siren
that's vanished in the air.
The stars
sing, and I am the knife
clipped to my front pocket
and my keys clipped to the back,
the dishes drying in the rack,
the cat's bowl, and the cat.

All My Life

Quiet friend who has come so far,
feel how your breath makes more space around you.
—Rainer Maria Rilke, "Sonnets to Orpheus"

I have lived where fog creeps
up the canyons,
and coyotes gather at dawn
(when I call to the owls
and they call back).
Here the wind strokes grass
like the strings of a fiddle,
and a multitude of songs
rise and fall in the fields
where the deer graze,
and the cougar hunts at dusk.
Here—where you can find
the broken bones of deer,
cow skulls, porous after years
under the sun and rain—
where the river is deepest,
if you drink from its banks
you find yourself
in the ripples and whirlpools,
rivulets running around rocks,
smooth river stones
beneath the water's surface,
scattered on the banks
overgrown with moss,
a place recognizable only
as the land of nowhere,
where the fog fills ravines
at night, and the stars
disappear.

What Is There To Know?

Light takes the trees; but who can tell us how?
—Theodore Roethke, "The Waking"

Despite my worldly wrongs
I sing, you're free

to go, not knowing where—here
I belong

beneath the sumac's twisting
leaves of green,

I walk and sing to name
what I have seen:

the thorny purple crowns
of bull thistle,

patches of common sunflowers
that gleam

in patches of sunlight breaking
through

this canopy of trees—
"How beautiful"

wrote Keats,
"are the retired flowers!"

made more so since
they do not name themselves.

The sinew of my muscles
spurs me on.

Sweat drips down my face
and clings like dew

upon the petals
of the goldenrod;

the Black-eyed Susans wilt
in this noon heat,

radiate discs, penny suns
that glow

beside the streams and shallow
creaks that flow

beneath the wooden bridges
that I cross.

I feel their waters coursing
through my veins,

the dappled light that creeps
across my chest;

we are one, the dust
of fallen stars,

pollen gathered from afar
that's come alive.

We breathe, and in a wink
we die. Between,

both cartographer and map,
we draw the lines

that sublimate
the actions of our lives,

which lead me round a bend
to this divide

where rows of maples
glitter in the wind;

their leaves, the gleaming
scales of fish beneath

the passing clouds, transformed
by light. Unseen,

rhythm and rhyme
live on in me—these sounds

resound within my skull
and yours as well

now. I am I as much as you
are you.

But who am I to say
where my self ends?

The same air fills our lungs,
their crossing veins;

entangle particles
may move as one.

A breath can last
a thousand years and more.

Our neurons mirror neurons
across synaptic plains—

this patterning of thought,
a symmetry.

Our breath is even
and our hearts beat

a steady rhythm
we both feel as I

cross an open field
this summer day

and sing of another's joy
that I have known:

the restless shimmering
of streams

hums within
the marrow of our bones,

the sweat that pearls
upon our skin, the salt

within, positive
and negatively charged

ionic compound,
crystals form

to make a geode
of each body where

there resonates
a polyphonic song

that vibrates
with the origin of myth.

It tells us to *Return.*
Return to breath.

Nocturnal Metempsychosis

Blessed art thou,
Who distinguishes holiness from the everyday.
—from the Havdalah

Surrounded by piles of books,
the spiral peel of a tangerine
at my feet, a bar of chocolate

open atop the nearest stack, I read
deep into the night, until my eyes won't
focus, and everything becomes

heavy—the books in their jackets,
the lids of my eyes, the air
pressing against every turned page,

even the orange of the spent rind
lies heavy in the glow of the lamp,
its light heavy. I return

the book to its stack, the chocolate
to its wrapper, leave
the shell of the tangerine,

turn off the lamp, and shuffle
towards sleep, untuck a corner
of my bed to settle

between the smooth cotton
sheets, a bookmark
fast in the center of a dream.

About the Author

Jake Young is the author of the poetry collection *American Oak* (Main Street Rag, 2018), the poetry chapbook *What They Will Say* (Finishing Line Press, 2021), and the essay collection *True Terroir* (Brandenburg Press, 2019). He received his MFA from North Carolina State University and his PhD from the University of Missouri. Young serves as the poetry editor for the *Chicago Quarterly Review*.

Made in the USA
Monee, IL
23 October 2021

79788562R00051